TOM BERLIN

RESTORED

FINDING REDEMPTION
IN OUR MESS

Youth Study Book
by Josh Tinley

Abingdon Press / Nashville

RESTORED
FINDING REDEMPTION IN OUR MESS
YOUTH STUDY BOOK

Copyright © 2016 Abingdon Press
All rights reserved.

This book is printed on elemental chlorine-free paper.

978-1-5018-2303-9

16 17 18 19 20 21 22 23 24 25—10 9 8 7 6 5 4 3 2 1
MANUFACTURED IN THE UNITED STATES OF AMERICA

CONTENTS

INTRODUCTION
LIFE IS MESSY, BUT GOD
HAS THINGS UNDER CONTROL

What comes to mind when you hear the word *mess*? Your room? Your schedule during a particularly busy week in the middle of the school year? Your love life? Messes are a part of being human and a part of living in a messy and broken world. Some messes are of our own doing; others are through no fault of our own. One way or another, our lives get messy.

The good news is that God is in the mess—not making the mess but working to redeem and restore it. God doesn't promise to eliminate messes from our lives, but God brings hope where there is despair, order where there is chaos. God blesses our messes and, in Christ, offers us grace for all situations.

This six-session study for youth takes a look at the messes we all deal with and examines how God redeems these messes and restores order. It is inspired by *Restored: Finding Redemption in Our Mess*, by Tom Berlin. Our study will have six sessions:

1. This Is a Real Mess
2. Who Left This Mess?
3. Bless This Mess
4. No Messing Around
5. Address This Mess
6. The Message in the Mess

You can do this study at any time of year, but it was written with the season of Lent in mind. Lent is a season of reflection and preparation, a time when we symbolically travel with Christ on his journey toward Jerusalem and the cross. Traditionally, Lent is also a time when people make commitments, whether to make a temporary sacrifice (such as giving up desserts) or to take on something new (such as reading one chapter from the Gospels each day during the season). The purpose of such commitments is to both grow spiritually and focus one's heart and mind on Christ. This study emphasizes taking on spiritual disciplines and other practices that will open you to God's transforming love and grace, whether during Lent or any other season.

Using This Book

Each session in *Restored: Youth Study Book* begins with a word study that explores in depth a term that is essential to that session. Some of these words may be familiar; others may be completely foreign. Regardless of your familiarity with the word, you should gain some insight into what the word means and how it applies to the key teaching for that session.

Following the opening word study, there are a variety of activities and discussion starters. You likely won't be able to complete all the activities in the allotted time, so pick and choose the activites that will work best for your group. Those activities that are most essential are marked with a double asterisk,** indicating that they are key activities. (Some of these key activities refer to and build on one another.) Next to each activity is an estimate of how long it will take and a list of necessary supplies, when applicable.

Every session closes with participants making two commitments: First, each person commits to actively doing one thing over the course of the next week. The task that a participant decides to do should be specific, measurable, and doable within the span of one week. Second, each person commits to a prayer focus for the week, something he or she will pray about each day. These commitments will be most effective if participants have an accountability partner who can check in with them throughout the week to see if they've been faithful to their commitments.

The hope is that, as you work through these six sessions, you will see glimpses of God's grace in messes that are otherwise frustrating. You will examine how God uses and transforms those parts of our lives that we otherwise don't appreciate.

1

THIS IS A REAL MESS

CLEANING OFF THE GRIME
FROM GOD'S MASTERWORKS

In this opening session, we will explore the importance of seeing the mess in our lives and understanding God's promise of restoration. Choose the activities that best fit the time you have available and the needs of your group, but place a priority on the key activities, which are marked with a double asterisk.

**Opening Word Study: Restore (10 minutes)

Supplies: Dry-erase board or paper, marker, online dictionary

During this session and over the next several weeks you will examine the idea of restoration. Before you get going, take some time to consider what the word *restore* actually means. Discuss:

**Key activities

- What comes to mind when you hear the words *restore* or *restoration*?
- How would you define the word *restore*?

Either as a group or in teams of three or four, come up with a definition of *restore* that you think would be suitable for a dictionary. Write down your definition(s) either on a dry-erase board or on paper.

Then look up the word *restore* in an online dictionary, such as Dictionary.com. The dictionary you use likely will have multiple definitions. For each definition, discuss:

- How does this definition compare with your definition(s)?
- Do you think that this definition refers to the type of restoration we'll be looking at in this study? Why or why not?

When you've gone through all the dictionary definitions, discuss:

- How do you think these definitions will relate to what we will talk about today and in the weeks ahead?

Open with the following prayer, or one of your own:

God of the mess, bless our time together today and in the weeks ahead. Give us the strength and courage to be honest with ourselves and with one another. Give us wisdom and patience as we discuss personal topics. And, as we learn together, remind us of your promise of restoration and new life. Amen.

Paint the Ceiling (15 minutes)

Supplies: Bibles, paper, markers, portable hard surfaces for drawing (such as clipboards or books), tape

Humans have found ways to restore all sorts of things: electronics, ecosystems, and reputations, to name a few. One area where our restoration skills are especially apparent is in the world of fine art. Painstaking work has gone into ensuring that artistic masterworks appear pristine. The frescoes gracing Rome's Sistine Chapel—including those on the ceiling painted by Michelangelo—have been the subject of one of humankind's most significant artistic restorations. In honor of Michelangelo's work on the chapel ceiling, which we have worked so hard to restore and preserve, try a little ceiling painting of your own.

Divide your group into pairs. (If you have an odd number of participants, have an adult leader pair off with someone.) Each pair should choose or be assigned one of the Scriptures listed after these instructions. (Pairs might select a Scripture reference out of a hat or container; a leader might assign a Scripture to each pair; or pairs might even choose their own Scriptures.)

Give each pair a sheet of paper and something hard and flat that they can attach the paper to, such as a clipboard, an individual dry-erase board, or a large hardcover children's book. Each pair also will need markers (or colored pencils or crayons). If you use books, make sure the markers won't bleed through the paper and damage the covers.

Each pair should read their Scripture and discuss how they might represent their Scripture visually, in drawing. Once the pair have an idea, one person should play the role of the artist; the other should play the role of the ceiling. The artist should lie flat on the floor. The "ceiling" should hold the paper and writing surface upside down above the artist. The artist then should make her or his best effort to represent the pair's Scripture in drawing.

After a couple of minutes, partners should switch roles. After a couple of more minutes, participants should stop (even if they aren't finished). Each pair should present their work to the group, summarizing the assigned Scripture and explaining how the pair chose to represent the Scripture artistically. Then ask:

- How did creating a visual representation of your assigned verses help you better understand and appreciate the Scripture?
- How does drawing on a surface that is above you compare with drawing on a table or easel? What makes it more difficult?

Scriptures:

- Exodus 16:13-21 (God provides food for the Israelites in the desert)
- 2 Kings 2:1-11 (Elijah ascends into heaven)
- John 11:38-46 (Jesus raises Lazarus)
- Acts 2:1-12 (Pentecost)

Make It Perfect Again (10 minutes)

Supplies: Old posters, tape, thumbtacks, markers or colored pencils

Beforehand gather some old posters. These could include store-bought posters or poster-sized work from a school art class. Choose posters with the knowledge that they probably won't survive this activity (at least not in their original state). Put strips of tape across the posters. You may use a variety of tapes: transparent tape, masking tape, duct tape, and so on. Also put some small holes in the posters using thumbtacks.

Divide participants into teams of three or four. Each team should take one of the posters and do as much as they can to restore it to its original state in five minutes. You will have to remove the tape. Regardless of how careful you are, some of the picture likely will come off with the tape. You will need to restore these spots using markers or colored pencils, re-creating the parts of the picture that have been torn away. You also will need to find a way to "fill in" any holes in the picture.

Discuss:

- What decisions did you have to make when you were restoring your posters?
- How, do you think, is the work that you did similar to and different from the work that professionals do when restoring classic works of art?
- What risks does one take when restoring a work of art?

Option: Show a video demonstrating how fine art is restored. Many such videos are available online, including some produced by art museums. Compare the crude techniques you used to restore your posters with the techniques used to restore the works of masters.

**Image of God (10 minutes)

Supplies: Bibles, camera phones

Read aloud Genesis 1:24-31, focusing on verse 27: "God created humanity in God's own image, in the divine image God created them." Discuss:

- What do you think it means to be created in God's image?
- There are billions of people on this planet, and we vary greatly in height, build, skin tone, hair color, and so forth. How is it possible that all of us are created in God's image?
- If being made in God's image is about something other than (or more than) physical appearance, what are some non-physical things that human beings have in common with God?

If time permits, also read aloud Psalm 8:1-5 and Psalm 139:13-14. Discuss:

- What do these Scriptures say about how God created us and who God created us to be?
- How do these Scriptures relate to the verses we read from Genesis?

Now read aloud Romans 3:23. Discuss:

- What does it mean that each of us has fallen "short of God's glory"?
- Genesis tells us that we were created in God's image. What happens to this image when we sin?

As a reminder of how sin distorts the perfect image of God in each one of us, every person should take two selfies: the first should be a normal picture with a nice smile; the second should be distorted in some way, such as by using an app that changes the image. (Such apps are available for free for smartphones.) You might have a leader take both pictures of every person then send them out by text message. You might have people make two lines and have a "normal photographer"

13

and a "distorted photographer." If resources permit, you also could print out everyone's pictures. One way or another, make sure that everyone gets two pictures. Encourage each person to keep their two pictures on their phones or other devices—or to keep the printouts in their wallets, purses, or Bibles—as reminders of how sin distorts the perfect image of God that is within each of them.

Before you move on, make sure everyone understands that, though we are all distorted by sin, the distortion of sin is not permanent.

The Truth Helps—Eventually (5 minutes)

Supplies: Bible

Group members should spend two minutes in silence, counting all the people of whom they have been critical, either verbally or mentally. They don't need to share their count with the rest of the group, but they should have an idea of how often they are critical of others.

Then read aloud Isaiah 64:6 (NIV): "All of us have become like one who is unclean, and all our righteous acts are like filthy rags; we all shrivel up like a leaf, and like the wind our sins sweep us away."

When we read verses like this one, it's probably easy for us to apply it to people we know. It's much more difficult to apply it to ourselves. While we can readily come up with reasons why others need to change, we don't always see the changes that are needed in our lives. Discuss:

- Are you familiar with the phrase "The truth hurts"? What is it about the truth that makes it hurtful?
- How hard is it to be honest with yourself about your sins and shortcomings?
- Why is it crucial that we be brutally honest with ourselves about the sin and mess in our lives?

Being completely honest with ourselves about the messiness of our lives can be painful, but it is a crucial step on the path to restoration and redemption. We have to be aware of our mess, and admit our mess, before we can open ourselves to God's grace and restoration.

**Own Your "Grime" (5 minutes)

Supplies: Bibles, a dry-erase board or large sheet of paper, marker

Bill Murray was one of the most successful comedic actors of the eighties and nineties, and has since played a number of critically acclaimed dramatic roles. Murray married Jennifer Butler in 1997, but the relationship ended in an ugly divorce eleven years later. Reflecting on his love life five years after the divorce, Murray explained that he wasn't ready to enter into a new relationship, saying:

> There's a lot that I am not doing that I need to do.... I don't have a problem connecting with people. My [issue] is connecting with myself.... What stops [any of us from connecting with ourselves] is we're kinda really ugly if we look really hard. We're not who we think we are. We're not as wonderful as we think we are.... It's hard.[1]

- What other celebrities do you know of who have been open about the "grime" in their lives and the changes they needed to make as a result?
- What events in your life have prompted you to focus on making changes?

Read Luke 18:9-14. Discuss:

- When in your life have you acted like the Pharisee in this story? When have you focused on other people's grime instead of focusing on your own?
- What do you think caused you to act like the Pharisee? What caused you to be so consumed with other people's shortcomings?
- When have you been like the tax collector, taking responsibility for the grime?

Brainstorm a list of tools that one can use to clean off grime from a surface, such as water, brushes, and cleaning products. After you have a good list, brainstorm a list of spiritual tools for removing grime. (The list could include things such as prayer, forgiveness, a Christian community, and so on.) Once you have a pretty good list of spiritual grime removers, discuss:

- How many of these tools are things that you provide to others?
- How many of these tools are things that other people give you?

Restored, Like the Sistine Chapel (10 minutes)

Supplies: Bibles, the posters from earlier in the session

We know that we all have grime that covers us and distorts the perfect image that God created. While there are things we can and should do to clean this grime, we are incapable by ourselves of fully restoring God's image in us. Read aloud the following Scriptures:

- Ephesians 2:8-10
- Colossians 2:13-14
- 1 Corinthians 15:50-55

Discuss:

- What do these verses say about how we are restored and made new?
- What role do we play in our restoration?
- What role does God play?

Refer back to the posters you restored earlier in the session.

- How does your restoration of these pictures compare to God's restoration of each of us?
- What is the goal of a professional who is restoring works of art? How is this different from the goal that God has when restoring us?
- What tools does God use to restore us?
- How does God work through us to restore one another?
- What does Ephesians 2:10 say about how God uses and works through us?

It is important to know that, while God is ultimately the only one who can fully restore us, we still have roles to play in God's work of restoration.

Fear and Shame (10 minutes)

Supplies: Bibles

Often, it is hard for us to be honest with ourselves and to show love for others because we are caught up in fear and/or shame. Discuss:

- When has fear caused you not to be honest with yourself or not to show love to someone else?
- What about shame? How has shame kept you from being honest with yourself or showing love to others?
- Why would fear keep us from being honest or fully loving others?
- Why would shame keep us from being honest or fully loving others?

Read aloud each of the following Scriptures. For each one, discuss these questions:

- What does this Scripture say about fear or shame?
- What does it say about how fear or shame affects our relationship with God?

Scriptures:

- Romans 8:14-15
- 1 John 4:18-21
- Genesis 3:1-24

**Wisdom from Philo (10 minutes)

Supplies: Bibles

The ancient Jewish Egyptian philosopher Philo of Alexandria is said to have said, "Be kind, for everyone you meet is waging a great battle." Read aloud this saying several times. Discuss:

- What do you think Philo meant by this saying?
- How would thinking about the battles and messes that each person is facing affect the way you treat that person?

Divide into teams of three or four and have each team select one of the people from the following list. Each of these people is someone whom we might be inclined to dislike or be unkind to. Rather than focus on what makes the people unlikeable, think about their "battles." What might these people be going through that causes them to act in a manner that upsets you? Teams should come up with a brief story about battles that the person might be facing.

- A driver weaves in and out of traffic, cutting off your family's car and nearly causing an accident.
- Someone you know seems to ignore you when you see him or her out in public.
- A teacher seems to have very little patience for his or her students while they are preparing for a big test.
- The cashier at a convenience store acts impolitely toward customers.

Allow each team to tell its story, then discuss:

- When you are upset with or annoyed by someone, do you ever stop to consider what that person might be going through?
- How would stopping to consider what "battles" these people might be facing affect how you treat and feel about them?
- Read John 9:1-7. What assumptions do Jesus' disciples make about the blind man? What are the dangers of making such assumptions?
- How might people think differently of you if they understood your "battles"?

We all have messes in our lives. Sometimes we are completely responsible for our messes, and sometimes we get into messes through no fault of our own. But often, messes are more complicated. Messes are the product of the sin and brokenness in the world. We all have a hand in it, and we all have a role to play in cleaning it up.

**Closing (5 minutes)

Gather in a circle. Allow everyone a minute or two in silence to think about the following two things:

- Something you'll do in the coming week in response to what you've learned and discussed in this session.
- Something you'll pray about in the coming week in response to what you've learned and discussed in this session.

For instance, you might commit to doing one nice thing per day for someone who is dealing with a particularly difficult battle or mess, and you might commit to praying each day for the courage to be honest about the mess in your own life.

Go around the circle and invite each person to name his or her two commitments for the week ahead. (As an option, have participants pair off with accountability partners who will check with them during the week to encourage them to keep up with their commitments.)

Close with this prayer or one of your own:

God the artist, thank you for doing the difficult work of restoring us, your creations. Guide us that we may be aware of the messes in our lives and sympathetic to the messes in the lives of others. Use us in your work of restoration so that we might participate in the perfection of your creation. Amen.

Chapter 1 Note

1. Julie Miller, "Bill Murray Explains Why He Doesn't Have a Girlfriend," *Vanity Fair*, October 2014 (http://www.vanityfair.com/hollywood /2014/10/bill-murray-girlfriend).

2

WHO LEFT THIS MESS?
MOVING BEYOND BLAME
AND CLAIMING GOD'S GRACE

In this second session, we look at how God is busy doing the hard work of redemption and restoration—cleaning up the messes that we all make—even before we are aware of it. Choose the activities that best fit the time you have available and the needs of your group, but place a priority on the key activities, which are marked with a double asterisk.

**Opening Word Study: Prevenient (10 minutes)

*Supplies: Dry-erase board or large sheet of paper, marker,
        online dictionary*

Write the word *prevenient* on a dry-erase board or large sheet of paper. Discuss:

**Key activities

21

- Do you have any familiarity with this word? If so, where have you encountered it? What do you think it means?

If you have access to a computer or tablet with Microsoft Word, type in the word *prevenient* and see if spellcheck accepts it. Then look up *prevenient* in an online dictionary. If it shows up, read aloud each of the definitions. Ask:

- Based on these definitions, what do you think this word has to do with the topic of our study: restoration? (*Participants who are familiar with the word and how it is used in some churches should probably be quiet.*)

Prevenient is a word that some Christians use to describe one way that God's grace works. And the idea of "prevenient grace" will be the focus of this session. But you'll come back to that in just a bit.

Before moving on, check in on how everyone did with the commitments they made as a part of the previous session. Were they faithful to their commitments? If so, what did they learn or gain? If not, why were they unable to stick to them?

Then open with the following prayer or one of your own:

God of grace, thank you for bringing us together for this time of study and fellowship. Open our hearts and minds to your guidance and instruction as we learn about and discuss the source of the mess in our lives and your promise of redemption. Amen.

**Who Made This Mess? (10 minutes)

Supplies: Dry-erase board or large sheet of paper, marker

As a group, identify anything about your meeting space that appears to be dirty, broken, out of place, or just off. This could include pencils that didn't make it back into the pencil can, carpet stains, torn paper on a bulletin board, and so forth. List these things on a dry-erase board or large sheet of paper. Then go through each item you've listed and ask, "Who made this mess?" You may have a clear, agreed-upon answer for some of the items; for other items, there may be disagreement; for still others, people may have no idea where the mess came from. Discuss:

- How important is it for us to know who is responsible for all the messes, blemishes, and misplaced items in this room?
- What is accomplished by placing blame?
- What are the dangers of dwelling too much on who is responsible for a mess?
- How responsible are we for fixing and cleaning up this mess?

Now make a second list, this time of the things that are broken and messy throughout the world. This could include natural disasters, wars, injustices, disputes, diseases, and so forth. Again, discuss who may be to blame for these messes, or whether it's even possible to blame anyone for some of them. Then answer these questions:

- How important is it for us to assign blame or responsibility for these messes? What is accomplished?
- What are the dangers of dwelling too much on who is to blame?
- What responsibility do we have for cleaning up these messes?

**Way, Way Back (15 minutes)

Supplies: Bibles, paper, pens or pencils

Participants should do their best to identify a time or moment when they first identified as a Christian. For some this may be a day they remember well when they accepted Christ into their lives. For others this may just be a time when they were old enough to understand why they went to church every week.

Every person should put together a timeline of significant events in their faith life leading up to the time or moment they have selected. These timelines might include items such as "My parents had me baptized"; "Started attending church"; "Met _____, who was a big influence on my faith"; "_____ invited me to attend a church function"; and so on. It's possible that some of the items on their timelines will stretch back to before they were born. Then read aloud the following Scriptures:

- Psalm 139:13-16
- Jeremiah 1:4-10

Discuss:

- What do these Scriptures have to say about the events leading up to us becoming Christians and responding to God's love?
- What do the Scriptures say about how God is at work in our lives before we are even aware of it?

Refer back to the word study from the beginning of this session. Some Christians refer to the grace of God that is working on us even before we know it as "prevenient grace." "Prevenient grace" describes how God seeks us and nudges us toward being in a relationship. For influential Christian thinkers Jacob Arminius and John Wesley, prevenient grace was key to their understanding of salvation and God's relationship with humankind. It remains an essential part of the beliefs of Methodist, Wesleyan, and Nazarene churches. Discuss:

- How have you experienced God's prevenient grace? What evidence of God do you see in your early life and before you were born?
- In what ways has God nudged you toward a life of faith?

And a Wee Little Man Was He (15 minutes)

Supplies: Bibles, Dry-erase board or large sheet of paper, marker

Discuss:

- What do you know about the story of Zacchaeus?

Allow those who are familiar with Zacchaeus to tell what they know of his story. Then read the story of Zacchaeus from Luke 19:1-10. How does the actual Scripture compare with what people had remembered? Then discuss the following questions:

- What do you know about tax collectors in Jesus' time? *(Tax collectors worked for the Roman government. They collected taxes that were owed, plus some extra so that they could make a living. Many people despised and distrusted tax collectors because they worked for the Romans—an outside empire that ruled Judea— and because they had a reputation for collecting much more than was necessary. A tax collector was also a key figure in Luke 18:9-14, one of the main Scriptures from Session 1, which precedes the story of Zacchaeus in Luke's Gospel.)*

- What do you think led Zacchaeus to become a tax collector? *(Scripture does not tell us, so all answers are speculation. But think about whether there might be a reason that makes Zacchaeus sympathetic.)*
- Why do you think Zacchaeus was so eager to see Jesus?
- What happened to Zacchaeus as a result of his decision to climb a tree and see Jesus?
- Why do you think Jesus decided to stay in the house of Zacchaeus, a tax collector?

Brainstorm a list of people (groups of people, not individuals) whom we might consider the equivalent of tax collectors today. What groups or occupations do we tend to distrust or assume the worst about? Briefly go through your list and discuss reasons why people view each group unfavorably. Talk about which reasons are fair and which are unfair. Then discuss:

- What are the dangers of making assumptions about someone based on that person's occupation or membership in a group?
- Are there ever valid reasons to have a negative opinion of people who do a particular job or belong to a particular organization? If so, what?

Option: Read Luke 19:8 from different translations, including the Common English Bible. Pay attention to the verb tenses. Does this verse suggest that Zacchaeus is going to give half his possessions to the poor and repay people he's cheated four times the amount? Or does it suggest that these are things that he already has been doing? How does changing the verb tense affect the meaning of the story?

In the Nick of Time (15 minutes)

Supplies: Bibles

Christian author Tom Berlin writes that "Jesus always seemed to show up at just the right time for people." Discuss:

- Do you agree with this statement? Why or why not?
- When in your life has Jesus shown up at just the right time?

When discussing the second question, keep in mind that Jesus gets involved in all sorts of ways, some of which we'd never expect. Jesus may intervene through a person, an opportunity, a sudden realization, or something wholly unexpected. There are no limits to how God can enter our lives.

To get a better appreciation of Jesus' timing, read through the following Scriptures. For each one, pay close attention to:

- The mess that people find themselves in
- How Jesus shows up at the perfect time to intervene

Scriptures:

- Mark 4:35-41
- Mark 5:21-42
- Luke 7:1-10
- John 8:2-11

Then discuss:

- How is Jesus' perfect timing related to the idea of God's prevenient grace, which you discussed earlier?

**How Does God Do It? (10 minutes)

Supplies: Dry-erase board or large sheet of paper, marker

God doesn't give up on us. Though we may give up on ourselves, God continues seeking us out and trying to get our attention. Even when we pull away from God, God calls us back. God wants us to understand that we're loved and valued—that we're forgiven and that we can be restored.

If you did the "Nick of Time" activity, you've already discussed times when Jesus intervened in your life at the perfect time. Now think about all the ways God could get someone's attention or intervene in someone's life. Consider examples from your earlier discussion, examples from Scripture, and examples from the stories of people you know. Record all of these examples on a dry-erase board or large sheet of paper. Then discuss:

- What do these examples tell us about how God works?
- What do these examples tell us about how God uses us to respond to life's messes?
- How does knowing this about God affect your attitude toward the messes you encounter, both in your life and in the lives of others?

You began this session with the question "Who made this mess?" Dwelling on who deserves the blame can be counterproductive and even destructive. God is invested in cleaning up the mess and invites us to participate in these efforts.

**Closing (5 minutes)

Gather in a circle. Allow everyone a minute or two in silence to think about the following two things:

- Something you'll do in the coming week in response to what you've learned and discussed in this session.
- Something you'll pray about in the coming week in response to what you've learned and discussed in this session.

You might think about situations where laying the blame on someone has kept you from forgiveness or from responding to a mess. (Note: Forgiving someone does not mean that the person is not at fault or that you should just excuse what that person has done. It does, however, mean moving forward and letting go of any grudges.) You might also think about people who are desperate to experience God in the midst of life's messes.

Go around the circle and invite each person to name his or her two commitments for the week ahead. (As an option, have participants pair off with accountability partners who will check with them during the week to encourage them to keep up with their commitments.)

Close with this prayer or one of your own:

God of grace, we know that we live in a messy world. Our lives our messy, and the people we encounter each day are struggling with messes of their own. Give us the strength and wisdom to move beyond placing the blame and to join in your work of redemption and restoration. Thank you for all the ways you have been present in our lives—all the ways you have stepped in at the perfect time. Work through us as you show your prevenient love and grace to all of your children. Amen.

3

BLESS THIS MESS

FINDING TRANSFORMATION AMID CHAOS

In this session we'll look at how God works within our messes to bring about transformation, both in our individual lives and for the entire world. No discussion of Christian transformation would be complete without looking at the Apostle Paul, whom God transformed from a persecutor of Christians into the leader of a mission that brought the message of Christ to all corners of the Roman Empire. Choose the activities that best fit the time you have available and the needs of your group, but place a priority on the key activities, which are marked with a double asterisk.

**Opening Word Study: Transformation (10 minutes)

Supplies: Dry-erase board or large sheet of paper, marker,
        online dictionary

**Key activities

When we are redeemed and restored, we are transformed. Open this session by exploring the idea of transformation.

- What comes to mind when you hear the word *transform* or *transformed*?
- How would you define the word *transform*?

Either as a group or in teams of three or four come up with a definition of *transform* that you think would be suitable for a dictionary. Write down your definition(s) either on a dry-erase board or on paper.

Then look up the word in an online dictionary, such as Dictionary. com. The dictionary you use likely will have multiple definitions. For each definition, discuss:

- How does this definition compare with your definition(s)?
- Do you think this definition refers to the type of transformation we'll be looking at in this study? Why or why not?

When you've gone through all the dictionary definitions, discuss:

- How do you think these definitions will relate to what we talk about today and in the weeks ahead?

Open with the following prayer, or one of your own:

God of transformation, bless our time together. Give us perseverance so that we will continue looking to you even when our messes seem overwhelming. Open our hearts and minds to the message you have for us today. Amen.

**How Well Do You Know Paul? (10 minutes)

Supplies: Something to keep score with
(Only do this activity if many in your group have spent significant time in Bible studies, Sunday school classes, or Bible classes at school.)

Paul is one of the most prominent figures in all of Scripture. In addition to playing a key role in the development of the early church, he also wrote many books of the New Testament. To test your knowledge of Paul, divide into two teams and run through the questions below.

Give one team a question. If that team answers correctly, it wins two points. If the team is incorrect, the other team may answer for one point. On true-or-false questions, the other team should not get an opportunity to steal. Answers to these questions can be found at the end of this session.

1. What city did Paul come from? In other words, he was known as Paul of _____.
2. Name five New Testament books, or letters, written by Paul.
3. Who was Paul's younger protégé? Two of Paul's New Testament letters were written to this person.
4. When he was young, Paul was present for and approved of the killing of what early Christian leader?
5. True or false: Paul used to be known as Saul, but God gave him a new name, "Paul," when he became a Christian.
6. True or false: Paul was one of Jesus' twelve disciples.
7. Many of the churches Paul started are in what current-day country that is partially in Europe and partially in Asia?
8. Paul's encounter with Christ occurred while he was on the road to what city, currently the capital of Syria?
9. True or false: Paul was Jewish.
10. True or false: Paul was a citizen of the Roman Empire.

Paul: The Movie (or Show or Game) (15 minutes)

Supplies: Paper, assorted art supplies

As a group, or as teams of three or four, come up with an idea for a movie, television series, or video game based on the life of Paul of Tarsus. This could be a literal retelling of his life, a modernization of his story, or an allegory. Present your idea in one of the following ways:

*   Script outline: A summary of each of the major events in Paul's story that will be presented on the show or in the game or movie

- Storyboard: A series of sketched drawings of key events and plot points in the show, game, or movie
- Trailer: A two-minute teaser that includes key scenes and a basic overview of the story and tells people why they should be interested in watching or playing

The Book of Acts gives a thorough account of Paul's life and ministry. When we meet him, he is persecuting Christians in Jerusalem. But after an encounter with Christ, Paul becomes an important and influential Christian apostle, starting churches and spreading the message of Christ throughout the Roman Empire. He encounters a lot of trials and messes along the way but eventually makes it to Rome, the capital of the empire. These Scriptures cover some of the key events in Paul's life:

- Acts 7:54–8:1 (Paul/Saul approves of the killing of Stephen, a Christian leader.)
- Acts 9:1-20 (Paul/Saul encounters Christ while traveling to Damascus to arrest Christians.)
- Acts 13 (Paul travels to preach and plant churches but faces opposition along the way.)
- Acts 15:1-21 (Paul successfully argues that the Jewish law should not apply to all the non-Jewish Christians who have joined the church as a result of his preaching.)
- Acts 16:16-34 (Paul ends up in prison and is released by a powerful earthquake, but not before introducing the jailer to Christ.)
- Acts 24:1-23, 27; 25:1-12 (Paul goes on trial before the Roman governors in Judea and appeals to Caesar in Rome.)
- Acts 27 (Paul travels to Rome but his ship wrecks.)
- Acts 28:11-31 (Paul arrives in Rome and begins his ministry in the capital of the known world.)

After you've put together your movie, show, or game idea, discuss:

- What messes did Paul encounter in his life?
- How was God at work in these messes?

One Word Is Not Enough (10 minutes)

Supplies: Paper, pens or pencils

The New Testament uses two different Greek words to refer to "life." One word, *bios*, refers to physical life. The other, *zoe*, refers to spiritual or eternal life. There are also two words for death: *teleute* means physical death, and *thanatos* means spiritual death. There are numerous other Greek words translated by multiple English words in our Bibles.

Divide into teams of three or four. Have each team identify an English word that might work better if it were more than one word. This might be a word that describes two or more completely different ideas; or it could be a word that describes one very rich and complex idea. Once you've selected a word, come up with additional words to describe other concepts contained within the original word. For instance, you may decide that the word *game* is insufficient to describe all types of games. So you might come up with one word to describe games that someone plays alone, a word to describe games where individuals play against one another, a word to describe team sports, and so on.

Allow each group to introduce its new words and to explain why they are necessary. Then discuss:

- Why might the Greek in which the New Testament is written use different words to describe life and death?
- What is the difference between *bios* (physical life) and *zoe* (spiritual, eternal life)?
- What is the difference between *teleute* (physical death) and *thanatos* (spiritual death)?
- Can a person be physically alive but spiritually dead? If so, what does this look like?
- For that matter, how can we be spiritually alive even when our physical lives are a mess?
- How can God work through physical messes to improve our spiritual health?

**Not Just the Little Things (5 minutes)

Discuss whether people in your group have ever committed to making changes for the season of Lent or for another occasion. These changes might have involved giving up a habit, committing to a spiritual practice, or setting aside regular time for service. After everyone has had a chance to think about and name these commitments, ask:

- For how long did you make the commitment?
- Were you able to stick with it?
- Did you continue this commitment over the long term? Why or why not?
- Did these changes have a long-term impact on your life? If so, how?

Small, temporary changes can draw us closer to God and enrich our faith, but the goal in our life is large-scale transformation. Discuss:

- How can little changes lead to bigger, more substantial changes? (For example, how can small changes keep us focused on the big picture?)
- How might small changes distract us from true transformation? (For example, how might small changes give us the feeling that we've been transformed even if we haven't?)

**Justified (10 minutes)

Supplies: Bible

In the previous session, you explored the idea of *prevenient grace*—the grace of God that was at work in your life even before you had an awareness of God. Another aspect of God's grace that many Christian thinkers have identified is *justifying grace*. Discuss:

- Based on what you've learned and discussed so far, would you say that humans are capable of restoring and redeeming ourselves?

- If we are not capable of taking care of our messes and brokenness, what hope do we have?

Thus far, we've discussed how God is the only one who can restore us and how God is hard at work cleaning up our messes even before we know there's a mess to clean up. Still, God wants us to participate in this work. God wants us to acknowledge our need for restoration and to invite God into our lives. Discuss:

- God loves us regardless of what we do. Why, then, is it important for us to accept God's love and grace?

Some people can identify a specific day or moment when they became aware of their need for God's grace and welcomed God into their hearts. For other people, this is a gradual process that may happen over the course of years. Invite volunteers who are comfortable doing so to talk about their experiences of accepting God's grace and welcoming God into their "mess."

Then read aloud Romans 5:1-5, which was written by the Apostle Paul, whom you may have studied earlier in this session. Discuss:

- What do these verses say about how we are saved, or "made righteous"?
- Based on these verses, what should our approach be to the messes we encounter?

**Stories of Blessed Messes (10 minutes)

Divide into pairs or groups of three. Each pair or group should come up with a well-known story that shows how God can use a mess to transform lives. These stories may be real or fictional. They might include a news story in which a group of people come together after a disaster or a movie where a character gains some great insight after going through a difficult trial.

Allow groups a few minutes to come up with a story. Then have each group talk about the selected story and why it is a good illustration of God's power to transform. Afterward discuss:

- How can stories such as these help us show other people how God is at work in our world?

Back to Paul (5 minutes)

(If you did the activities related to Paul earlier in this session, revisit Paul's story in light of the other things you've learned and discussed.)

Discuss:

- What were some of the messes in Paul's life? How do you think God was at work in these messes?
- How did Paul experience God's justifying grace? In other words, when and how did Paul become aware of his "mess" and his need for restoration?
- What messes did Paul encounter even after he accepted Christ into his life? How did he approach these messes?

**Closing (5 minutes)

Gather in a circle. Allow everyone a minute or two in silence to think about the following two things:

- Something you'll do in the coming week in response to what you've learned and discussed in this session.
- Something you'll pray about in the coming week in response to what you've learned and discussed in this session.

For instance, you might commit to reading one chapter each day from the Book of Acts about Paul's life and ministry, and you might commit to praying each day for those who need to experience God's love in a personal way.

Go around the circle and invite each person to name his or her two commitments for the week ahead. (As an option, have participants pair off with accountability partners who will check with them during the week to encourage them to keep up with their commitments.)

Close with this prayer or one of your own:

Lord, we know that one of the most influential people in Christian history was a mess, and you used him to transform others. Open our eyes so that we can see how you are present in our messes; and open our hearts so that we may be transformed by your justifying grace and so that you might use us for the transformation of the world. Amen.

Answers to "How Well Do You Know Paul?"

1. Tarsus
2. Any five from: Romans, 1 Corinthians, 2 Corinthians, Galatians, Ephesians, Philippians, Colossians, 1 Thessalonians, 2 Thessalonians, 1 Timothy, 2 Timothy, Titus, Philemon
3. Timothy
4. Stephen
5. False: "Paul" and "Saul" are two renderings of the same name. Jewish people knew him mostly as "Saul"; Greeks knew him largely as "Paul."
6. False: While Paul was an apostle, he was not one of the twelve who traveled with Jesus during Jesus' earthly ministry.
7. Turkey
8. Damascus
9. True: Paul was Jewish and trained under the famous rabbi Gamaliel, but after becoming a Christian he didn't think that non-Jewish Christians should have to follow the Jewish law.
10. True: Paul used his status as a Roman citizen to better communicate to Greek and Roman audiences.

4

NO MESSING AROUND
LIVING A NEW, UNCOMFORTABLE
LIFE IN CHRIST

In this session, we'll look at the new life we have through Christ. Christians talk a lot about new life and being born again, but we don't always take seriously what this new life should look like. Choose the activities that best fit the time you have available and the needs of your group, but place a priority on the key activities, which are marked with a double asterisk.

**Opening Word Study: Sin (10 minutes)

Supplies: Dry-erase board or large sheet of paper, marker,
online dictionary

**Key activities

Sin is an important concept for Christians. It's a word we use a lot. How we understand sin affects how we live and how we understand salvation. But what is sin?

Either as a group or in teams of three or four, come up with a definition of *sin* that you think would be suitable for a dictionary. Write down your definition(s) either on a dry-erase board or on a large sheet of paper.

Then look up the word in an online dictionary, such as Dictionary. com. The dictionary you use likely will have multiple definitions. For each definition, discuss:

- How does this definition compare with your definition(s)?
- Do you think this definition refers to the type of sin we'll be looking at in this study? Why or why not?

When you've gone through all the dictionary definitions, discuss:

- How do you think these definitions will relate to what we talk about today and in the rest of this study?

Open with the following prayer, or one of your own:

God of goodness, bless our time together today as we come to terms with the reality of sin. As we discuss difficult topics and uncomfortable truths, keep us focused on the good news of your love and grace. Amen.

Goal Setting (15 minutes)

Supplies: Dry-erase board or large sheet of paper, markers

Divide into pairs or teams of three, and challenge each team to come up with an answer to the question, "What is the goal of the Christian life?" Teams and pairs should focus on a Christian's earthly life. In other words, the answer can't simply be "to get to heaven."

Give teams a few minutes to discuss, then invite each team to give its answer. Record these on a dry-erase board or a large sheet of paper. Then discuss:

- To what extent are these goals that you work toward?
- What sorts of things do you do to reach these goals?

For each of the goals that you come up with, identify three or four short-term goals that, if met, could bring you closer to meeting the larger goal. (For instance, if the goal of the Christian life were to win an Academy Award for Best Director, short-term goals might include directing an original short film or getting accepted to a film school.) When you have short-term goals for each long-term goal, discuss:

- Which of these short-term goals can you meet or work toward right now?
- What can you do to meet these short-term goals?

**The Price of Sin (10 minutes)

Supplies: Dry-erase board or large sheet of paper, marker

There are different ways to describe the goal of the Christian life, but one way or another we seek new life with Christ. We can live into this new life here and now, but how do we know if are truly living new life with Christ?

One way to know whether we've stepped into this new life is that we become more aware of the price, or impact, of our sin.

Allow a couple minutes for everyone to reflect silently on how sin has been present in their lives—both the sins they have commited and the sin in the world around them that has had an impact on their lives.

Following this time of reflection, ask:

- Think of all the sins you've identified. What are the effects of these sins on you personally?
- What are the effects of these sins on those around you?
- What are the effects of these sins on the world as a whole?

Then brainstorm some sinful things that someone your age might be tempted to do. Be as specific as possible. (Try to avoid vague answers such as "Being selfish," and instead give examples of being selfish such as "Ignoring someone who is hurting.") Record examples on a dry-erase board or a large sheet of paper.

Go through the items on your list. For each one, discuss:

- What makes this sin so tempting?
- When you are tempted to commit this sin, do you consider the impact it will have on your life? The impact it will have on the lives of others?
- What is the cost of this sin for you (the person guilty of it)?
- What is the cost of this sin for other people?
- How might considering the cost of this sin affect how you react when you are tempted?

**Don't Go It Alone (10 minutes)

Supplies: Bibles, a wall

A second way to know that we have entered into a new life with Christ is to recognize that we are powerless on our own to change ourselves. Illustrate this idea with the following activity. (You may choose to have one person do this activity as a demonstration, or you can allow everyone to try.)

Stand next to a wall so that your head, right shoulder, right knee, and right ankle are touching the wall. Then try to lift your left leg without moving your head, shoulder, knee, or ankle from the wall. In all likelihood, you won't be able to do it.

While you can't do this on your own, you can do it if you have help. Try the exercise again, this time with someone to assist you. Following this exercise, ask:

- What are some other things that you are incapable of doing on your own that you would be able to do with assistance?
- What problems can we get into when we assume that we can take care of things on our own?
- When have you gotten into trouble by trying to do too much on your own?

Read each of the following Scriptures. Discuss what each one says about how we rely on God for our salvation.

- Romans 3:9-24 (You read part of this Scripture in an earlier session.)
- Galatians 3:10-14
- Ephesians 2:1-10 (You also read part of this Scripture in an earlier session.)

Then discuss:

- How does knowing that we cannot overcome sin on our own—and that we rely entirely on God for our salvation—affect our faith and how we live our lives?

**Born All Over Again (15 minutes)

Supplies: Bibles, dry-erase board or large sheet of paper, marker

Brainstorm words and phrases that people associate with giving birth. If participants have trouble coming up with ideas, have them think about scenes from movies or television shows in which a character gives birth. (Granted, these scenes aren't always accurate, but most do convey the stress, urgency, and discomfort of the situation.) List these on a dry-erase board or a large sheet of paper.

After a few minutes of brainstorming, circle any words or phrases related to pain and discomfort.

Note: If someone in your group has given birth, talk with her beforehand and invite her, if she is willing, to describe briefly the pain and discomfort she experienced. Be sensitive to her experience when discussing this topic.

Then ask:

- What do you think the birthing process is like for the baby? (Keep in mind that the baby is going from a dark, secure environment to a bright, open-air environment full of sensory stimulation.)

All of us came into this world through a process that is painful and chaotic and traumatic for all involved. And Jesus tells us that we have to do it again.

Read John 3:1-18. Discuss:

- What does Nicodemus not understand about being "born again" or "born anew"?
- How familiar are you with the concept of being "born again"? In your mind, what does it mean to be born again?
- What, according to Jesus, do we have to do to be reborn? (It is important to remember that God is the one responsible for our rebirth. We merely accept God's grace.)
- What things change when we are born again? How might those things be jarring or uncomfortable, much like physical birth?
- How does this discussion about being reborn relate to the other things you've talked about in this session?

We are born again into a new life in Christ, a life in which we realize the costs of our sin and in which we know we are powerless to eliminate our sin. On the surface, this seems like a bad situation to be in. But we serve a God who lived on earth as a human being, who knows our limitations, who has defeated sin and death, and who has promised to be present with us always.

Salvation Fill in the Blanks (15 minutes)

Supplies: Bibles, scrap paper, nice paper, pens and pencils or markers

Divide into teams of three or four. Each team should read Ephesians 2:1-10 (which you already read as a part of "Don't Go It Alone") and work to fill in the blanks below.

1. All of us were once like dead people because of our _____.
2. We are saved for a new life with Christ by _____.
3. Salvation is a _____.

44

4. It is not something that we _____.
5. God saves us from _____.
6. God saves us for _____.

After teams have had a couple of minutes to work, they should check their answers with other teams. Suggested answers can be found at the end of this session, though answers other than those listed may also be acceptable.

Once you've gone through the answers, teams should summarize Ephesians 2:1-10 in three or fewer sentences. Each team should work out a summary on scrap paper and then, when finished, write it in large letters on a nice sheet of paper. Hang these summaries in your meeting space as a reminder of the good news of salvation through Christ.

**Closing (5 minutes)

Gather in a circle. Allow everyone a minute or two in silence to think about the following two things:

- Something you'll do in the coming week in response to what you've learned and discussed in this session.
- Something you'll pray about in the coming week in response to what you've learned and discussed in this session.

For instance, you might keep a journal where you note the effects of sin—both in your personal life and in the world around you. You might commit to praying for those who are adjusting to the shock of being born into a new life in Christ.

Go around the circle and invite each person to name his or her two commitments for the week ahead. (As an option, have participants pair off with accountability partners who will check with them during the week to encourage them to keep up with their commitments.)

Close with this prayer or one of your own:

God of new life, thank you for the promise of new, eternal life that we have through Christ. Guide us through the discomfort and uncertainty of this new life. Give us the courage to be honest about our sins and the wisdom to be aware of the effects of our sins. Give us the humility to recognize that we cannot overcome sin on our own but rely entirely on your grace and mercy. Amen.

Answers to "Salvation Fill in the Blanks"

1. Sin or offenses against God or disobedience
2. God's grace or God's mercy
3. Gift
4. Earn or possess or should be proud of
5. Sin or death
6. Good things or good works

5

ADDRESS THIS MESS
GROWING CLOSER TO CHRIST THROUGH DISCIPLINE

In this session we will explore the topic of spiritual discipline and spiritual disciplines. Choose the activities that best fit the time you have available and the needs of your group, but place a priority on the key activities, which are marked with a double asterisk.

**Opening Word Study: Discipline (10 minutes)

Supplies: Dry-erase board or large sheet of paper, marker,
online dictionary

The focus of this section is spiritual disciplines. Before getting into spiritual disciplines and why they are important, examine the word *discipline* and what it really means. Discuss:

**Key activities

- What comes to mind when you hear the word *discipline*?
- How would you define the word *discipline*?

Either as a group or in teams of three or four come up with a definition of *discipline* that you think would be suitable for a dictionary. Write down your definition(s) either on a dry-erase board or on paper.

Then look up the word in an online dictionary, such as Dictionary. com. The dictionary you use likely will have multiple definitions. For each definition, discuss:

- How does this definition compare with your definition(s)?
- Do you think this definition refers to the type of discipline that we'll be looking at in this session? Why or why not?

When you've gone through all the definitions, ask:

- How do you think these definitions will relate to what we talk about today?

Open with the following prayer, or one of your own:

God of growth, give us discipline today as we evaluate our habits and practices. Open our minds and ears to the wisdom of our peers and give us the courage to be honest about the junk that clutters our life. In Jesus' name we pray. Amen.

The Junk Drawer (10 minutes)

Ask:

- Do you have a drawer, cabinet, or closet in your house that is set aside mostly for junk? If so, what sorts of things end up in this cabinet or drawer? How did you choose this space to be the place for junk? Did your family specifically set it aside as the "junk drawer," or did it just assume this role over time?
- How do new items end up in the junk drawer?
- Have you ever thrown things in the junk drawer (or closet or cabinet) to avoid putting them where they actually belong? Why did you do this?

Often when we straighten up our homes or rooms, we just stuff things into drawers and closets instead of properly putting them away. Doing this gives the impression that the room or house is clean when it actually isn't.

- How do you do this in your life? How do you give the impression that everything is okay and under control, even when it isn't?
- What sorts of things do you try to hide away so you don't have to deal with them?
- What are the effects of never cleaning out the junk drawer in your house?
- What are the effects of never dealing with the things in your life that you've hidden away?

Unclean Your Room (10 minutes)

Supplies: Bibles, paper, pens or pencils or markers

Each person should make a diagram of his or her bedroom in its cleanest state. It should include any furniture, lamps, and anything else that sits on the floor permanently. Once people have completed their diagrams, they should start to add items that might end up on the floor (or the bed or the desk) after the room has been cleaned. Everyone should continue to add items to the room until it resembles what it would look like before being cleaned.

Invite volunteers to present their diagrams and talk about the items that end up on their floors and desks and beds, which clutter their rooms after they've been cleaned. Ask:

- When you clean your room, do you make a goal or promise to keep it clean for an extended period of time?
- After you clean your room, how long does it take before the room once again looks like your messy diagram?
- Why does your room inevitably get messy again, no matter how much you want to keep it clean?

Throughout this study, we've looked at the topic of transformation. We've looked at short-term tranformations and the difficulty of sustaining them. Like our rooms, our lives inevitably get messy again.

Read the following Scriptures:

- Mark 10:17-27
- Romans 7:13-25

Discuss:

- What do these Scriptures tell us about our ability to transform our own lives?
- Where can we find hope, according to these Scriptures?

**Do's and Don'ts (5 minutes)

Supplies: Dry-erase board or large sheet of paper, marker, notepads, pens or pencils

Divide participants into groups of three or four. Have each group create two lists of rules for being a part of your youth group / Sunday school class / small group / Bible study. In one list, all the rules should begin with "do." In the other list, all the rules should begin with "don't." For instance, one of the rules in the first list might be, "Do give the group your full attention"; a rule in the second list might be, "Don't dominate the conversation by talking incessantly."

Spend a few minutes compiling these lists. Then read all the rules aloud and record them on a dry-erase board or a large sheet of paper. You don't all need to agree on every single rule, but if time permits, amend and delete rules so you have a list that most people are comfortable with. Then ask:

- If everyone were to be faithful to all these rules, what effect would it have on our group?
- Why is it important to have rules and guidelines to follow?

- What is the value in having both "do's" and "don'ts" on the list? How might the list be inadequate if it were only one or the other?

The importance of both do's and don'ts will figure into your discussion of spiritual disciplines.

**Make It a Habit (10 minutes)

Supplies: Scrap paper, pens or pencils

Now hand out scrap paper and ask everyone to make a list of things that have become habits—things they do daily, frequently, or incessantly no matter what. While *habit* sometimes has a negative connotation ("bad habits"), this could include things such as brushing your teeth, washing your face, taking out the trash, doing homework at a certain time of day, getting to school early, and so forth. Next to each item on the list, participants should make a note of about how long this habit has been a part of their lives.

After everyone has had a few minutes to work, discuss:

- Which habits have been a part of your life for the longest?
- How did these longtime habits develop? How did they become habits?
- How would your life be different (for worse or better) if these habits were not a part of it?
- What about spiritual habits? Are there spiritual habits that are a part of your daily or weekly routine? If so, what are they? What, if anything, is different about these habits?

**The Discipline to Say No (10 minutes)

Supplies: Paper, pens or pencils; online dictionaries may be helpful

In previous sessions, we discussed how we are incapable of overcoming sin and living a new life with Christ on our own. We rely entirely on God's love and grace. This does not mean we're entirely powerless. We can reject God's grace, or we can open ourselves to it. One way we open ourselves to God's grace is through spiritual disciplines. Ask:

- What comes to mind when you hear the phrase "spiritual disciplines"?

Spiritual disciplines are practices that focus our minds and hearts on God's will. Much like our lists of do's and don'ts, we can put spiritual disciplines into two categories: Disciplines of Abstinence and Disciplines of Engagement. Disciplines of Abstinence are the "don'ts"—the things we don't do because we claim our identities as God's children. Disciplines of Engagement are the "do's"—the things we do in response to God's love.

Disciplines of Abstinence include (among other things):

- Solitude
- Silence
- Frugality
- Chastity
- Sacrifice[1]

Talk about whether people are familiar with these words. If they are not, discuss their meaning, consulting online dictionaries as needed. Then discuss:

- How might practices such as solitude and silence bring us closer to God?
- How might practices involving sacrifice (whether that means sacrificing behaviors or sacrificing material things) help you grow in your relationship with Christ?

As a group or in teams of three or four, make a list of things that someone could give up—either partially or entirely—to grow in faith. Once you have a good list, discuss any items that people aren't sure about. Then ask:

- Which of these things could you abstain from, either partially or entirely?
- How would giving up or letting go of these things help you grow in your relationship with Christ?

Challenge one another to identify one thing to let go of during the coming week. While it is good to eliminate things such as greed and arrogance, for the purposes of this activity you should choose something tangible. You may consider giving up a certain type of junk food, especially if you are spending a lot of money on it; you might abstain from a particular video game that is occupying a large amount of your time; or you might look at staying away from an online forum where you are often tempted to post hurtful messages.

Invite volunteers to talk about what they're going to let go of. Then ask:

- How will letting go of this thing affect your relationships with others? your relationship with God?
- How difficult would it be to cut back on this thing over the long term or eliminate it entirely? Do you think it would be in your best interests to do so?

**The Discipline to Say Yes (10 minutes)

Supplies: Paper, pens or pencils; online dictionaries may be helpful

In addition to Disciplines of Abstinence, there are also Disciplines of Engagement, which include (among others):

- Study
- Worship
- Celebration
- Service
- Prayer
- Fellowship
- Confession[2]

Talk about whether people are familiar with these words. If they are not, discuss their meaning, consulting online dictionaries as needed. Then discuss:

- Which of the practices do you already do regularly?
- Which would you like to do more often than you already do?
- What do you think is the value of disciplines such as celebration and fellowship (spending time in the company of other Christians)?

As a group or in teams of three or four, make three lists: one of Disciplines of Engagement someone could do daily; one of Disciplines of Engagement someone could do weekly; and one of Disciplines of Engagement one could do periodically (a couple of times a month or a few times a year). Don't limit yourself to the disciplines listed above. Feel free to be more specific (for instance, particular types of service) or to include additional spiritual practices.

Look over your list(s). Then discuss:

- How do these things help you grow in your relationships with one another? How do they help you grow in your relationship with Christ?
- Which of these practices could become habits?
- What might you need to change or eliminate to make these Disciplines of Engagement more a part of your life?

Martha's Mess, Mary's Mess (10 minutes)

Supplies: Bibles

Read Luke 10:38-42, the story of Jesus' visit with Mary and Martha. Select one person in your group to play the role of Mary and one to play the role of Martha. Mary and Martha should have a short debate in which each one tries to show that she acted correctly during Jesus' visit. Martha should justify her decision to tend to the household chores; Mary should justify her decision to sit at Jesus' feet, listening.

After the debate, discuss:

- Which sister do you think was correct in this situation? Why?
- Which sister do you identify with more closely? Why?

- What mess was Martha tending to? What "mess" was Mary tending to?

Martha had many tasks that distracted her from focusing on Jesus. In our time together, we looked at things that distract us from our relationship with Christ (such as Martha's tasks) and things that help us to give Jesus our full attention (as Mary did). Discuss:

- What are some things you can do to become more like Mary, with your attention fully focused on Christ?
- How can the disciplines we've explored in this session help you be more like Mary?

**Closing (5 minutes)

Gather in a circle. Allow everyone a minute or two in silence to think about the following two things:

- Something you'll do in the coming week in response to what you've learned and discussed in this session.
- Something you'll pray about in the coming week in response to what you've learned and discussed in this session.

For this session you may already have made some commitments or come up with some ideas related to spiritual disciplines; you might consider praying about priorities and staying focused.

Go around the circle and invite each person to name his or her two commitments for the week ahead. (As an option, have participants pair off with accountability partners who will check with them during the week to encourage them to keep up with their commitments.)

Close with this prayer or one of your own:

God of discipline, we are distracted by many things and struggle to stay focused on you and your will for us. Give us the patience and perseverance to develop spiritual habits so that we will grow in faith. And give us the self-control to eliminate habits that are destructive or that may become distractions. Amen.

Chapter 5 Notes

1. Dallas Willard, *The Spirit of the Disciplines: Understanding How God Changes Lives* (New York: HarperCollins, 1991), 158.

2. Ibid.

6

THE MESSAGE IN THE MESS
LOVING GOD AND NEIGHBOR

As you've gone through this study, you've learned about God's prevenient grace and justifying grace. In this final session, we will learn about a third movement of God's grace. Choose the activities that best fit the time you have available and the needs of your group, but place a priority on the key activities, which are marked with a double asterisk.

**Opening Word Study: Sanctify (10 minutes)

Supplies: Dry-erase board or large sheet of paper, marker, online dictionary

One of the key terms that you'll be discussing in this final session is *sanctification*. Before you start, take some time to explore the meaning of the word *sanctify*. Discuss:

**Key activities

- What comes to mind when you hear the word *sanctify* or *sanctification*?
- How would you define the word *sanctify*?

Either as a group or in teams of three or four, come up with a definition that you think would be suitable for a dictionary. Write down your definition(s) either on a dry-erase board or on paper.

Then look up the word in an online dictionary, such as Dictionary.com. The dictionary you use likely will have multiple definitions. For each definition, discuss:

- How does this definition compare with your definition(s)?
- Do you think this definition refers to the type of sanctification we'll be looking at in this study? Why or why not?

When you've gone through all of the dictionary definitions, discuss:

- How do you think these definitions will relate to what we talk about today?

Open with the following prayer, or one of your own:

Holy God, bless our final session together. Guide our discussion as we bring our study of messes and restoration to a conclusion. May the knowledge and insight we gain during our time together stick with us as we continue growing in faith. Amen.

**Write the History Books (10 minutes)

Supplies: Paper, pens or pencils

Discuss:

What does the word *legacy* mean to you?
- In what situations and contexts do you hear people talk about "legacy"?

Often when a great athlete, entertainer, or political figure nears the end of his or her career, fans, pundits, and critics discuss and debate the legacy that this person will leave. What accomplishments or shortcomings will the person most be remembered for? Will he or she go down as one of the all-time greats, or as one of the all-time disappointments?

Thanks to technology, there is no limit to the amount of information we can leave for future generations. Even those of us who don't become world-famous will leave a lasting legacy. Imagine that someone one hundred years from now is writing a paragraph in an electronic encyclopedia (or whatever exists then) about your life and legacy. What will that paragraph say?

Spend only a few minutes writing, and make sure you don't write more than four or five sentences. Allow volunteers to read aloud their encyclopedia entries. Then discuss:

- How important is it to you that people remember you long after you are gone?
- What does the word *legacy* mean to you? How important to you is the legacy that you leave?
- We obviously don't remember most of the people who have lived before us. How have these people nonetheless had an impact on our world today?
- Why is the legacy we leave important, regardless of whether people remember us personally?

**Most Important? (10 minutes)

Supplies: Bibles, paper, pens or pencils

The Bible contains literally hundreds of rules and commandments. If someone were to ask you, "What does the Bible tell me to do?" it would be impossible to cover everything. But you could summarize.

Divide into teams of three or four. Each team should spend a few minutes writing a two-sentence summary of the Bible's teachings. The objective is to come up with two sentences that get at the heart of how God, as shown through the Bible, wants Christians to live.

Allow each team to read aloud its summary. After each one, discuss:

- What do you like about this summary?
- What, if anything, is missing from this summary?

After going through all the summaries, ask:

- Which summary do you think best summarizes the Bible's teachings?
- Is it possible to summarize adequately all of God's commandments in two sentences? Why or why not?

Scripture has some summaries of its own. Read the following Scriptures. For each one, discuss:

- How do these verses summarize God's commandments?

Scriptures:

- Matthew 22:34-40
- Galatians 5:13-15

**At the Highest Level (10 minutes)

Supplies: Electronic devices with Internet access

Each person should select an activity which she or he would like to perform at a high level, such as a sport or performing art. Every participant then should spend a few minutes researching on an electronic device what it would take to do this activity at the highest level. For instance, one might look at how many French horn players can get jobs with a major symphony orchestra. One might find out the times one would need in order to compete in the Olympics as a swimmer or runner. One might learn the training, protocols, and preparation one must go through to climb Mount Everest.

Participants with similar interests may team up. (This may be necessary if there are not enough electronic devices for each person.)

After a few minutes, invite volunteers to talk about what they found. Then discuss:

- If you really want to be successful at the highest levels of these activities, what sorts of things will you need to do?
- How long would it take you to reach that level?

Even though salvation in Christ isn't something we earn, it is still something we can work toward and get better at. We do this by focusing on the end goal of following the two greatest commandments: loving God and loving neighbor. Discuss:

- In your life thus far, how have you made progress toward the end goal of fully loving God and neighbor?
- What sorts of things can we do to grow in faith toward the goal of fully loving God and neighbor? (Consider what you discussed in previous sessions about spiritual discipline.)
- How does this discussion relate to our key word, *sanctify*?

**Grace and Grace and Grace Again (5 minutes)

Discuss:

- In other sessions you looked at two movements of God's grace—two ways that Christian thinkers have identified God's grace at work in our lives. What were they? *(As needed, look back to previous sessions.)*
- How does God work through these two types of grace?

A third movement of God's grace that Christian thinkers have identified is "sanctifying grace." After God's Holy Spirit has nudged us toward a relationship with Christ (prevenient grace) and opened our hearts to accept Christ's love (justifying grace), God then works to move us toward perfection through sanctifying grace. Sanctifying grace reminds us that God is present with us and is active in our lives. We experience this grace when we feel moved to spend time with God, gain a greater understanding of God's will, and grow closer to God. It often shows itself in spiritual disciplines.

Discuss:

- To sanctify means to "make holy." In what ways does God make us holy?
- When and where do you feel closest to God?
- What habits and activities draw you closer to God and give you a better understanding of God's will?

Love or Infatuation? (10 minutes)

Choose three volunteers to be characters in a role-play. In this situation, two of the characters will be "in love" with the third. The first of the "in love" characters should truly love and care about the person; the second "in love" person should just be infatuated with the third. The rest of the group should be the audience.

The audience should call out situations in which the characters might find themselves. The characters should then act out those situations. While they're acting, the first character should demonstrate sincere love and concern for the third. The second should be concerned mainly about how the third person makes him or her feel. (For instance, if the characters are sitting around talking at a restaurant, the first character might be asking questions about the third person's life and listening intently; the second character, on the other hand, might be upset because the third person isn't paying attention to him or her.)

Act out a few different situations. Then discuss:

- What is the difference between truly loving someone or something and just being infatuated with someone or something?
- What sorts of things can we do (and do we do) to show genuine love to God?
- What sorts of things do we do that are the product of being infatuated, or of being a Christian for selfish reasons?

The Bible uses different words for love, but the word that describes love of God—and God's love for us—is *agape* (uh-GAH-pay). This kind of love isn't just a feeling. It involves full devotion, and it shows itself in our actions.

Discuss:

- What can we do (and do we do) to have this active *agape* love for God?

Go Fly a Kite! (20 minutes)

Supplies: Kites

Note: You may want to do this activity outside of your regular meeting time, possibly immediately before or after.

If weather and space permit, go outside and try your hand at flying a kite. If members of your group own good kites, you may use them, but you should be able to find inexpensive kites at a dollar or discount store. (These cheap kites might not be very durable but they should suit this activity.)

Fly kites in pairs. One person should hold the actual kite while the other holds the reel. The person with the kite should walk away from the reel while the person with the reel unravels about twenty yards of string. The person holding the kite should wait for a gust of wind and then release the kite into the air. Once the kite is in the air, the person with the reel should release more string to get more altitude. This person may also need to change position as the wind changes direction. (There are many resources available online that show how to fly a kite.)

Afterward, discuss your kite-flying experience, what went well and what was frustrating. You probably discovered that the most important factor in successfully flying a kite is the wind. While you cannot control the wind, you can choose to fly the kite at times and in places when and where a strong wind is likely.

Flying a kite is similar to having a relationship with the Holy Spirit. Much as we can't control the kite in the sky, we also can't control the Holy Spirit. But, as we put ourselves in position to catch a gust of wind that will send our kite high into the sky, we also can position ourselves in the flow of the Spirit. Discuss:

- How do we position ourselves in the flow of the Holy Spirit? (Think about the spiritual disciplines you discussed in the previous session.)
- What does this have to do with sanctifying grace?

**Closing (5 minutes)

Gather in a circle. Allow everyone a minute or two in silence to think about the following two things:

- Something you'll do in the coming week in response to what you've learned and discussed in this session.
- Something you'll pray about in the coming week in response to what you've learned and discussed in this session.

For instance, you might make a commitment to do one specific thing to show love to God and one specific thing to show love to your neighbors, and you might pray that you may show genuine love and not just infatuation.

Go around the circle and invite each person to name his or her two commitments for the week ahead. (As an option, have participants pair off with accountability partners who will check with them during the week to encourage them to keep up with their commitments.)

Close with this prayer or one of your own:

God of grace, thank you for being present with us during this study. Give us the strength to stay true to the commitments we've made and the persistence to develop holy habits in response to what we've learned. Bless each person in our group going forward. Amen.

CPSIA information can be obtained
at www.ICGtesting.com
Printed in the USA
LVHW082040310120
645512LV00005B/43